THIS BOOK
BELONGS TO:

_____

_____

_____

INTRODUCTION

Welcome to a journey of faith, hope, and manifestation tailored uniquely for our cherished Black Christian family. In this Vision Board Clip Art Book, we invite you to embark on a transformative experience that celebrates our spiritual journey, embraces our faith, and ignites our dreams.

We understand the power of vision and the importance of grounding our aspirations in the promises of God. In a world filled with worldly distractions, it's vital for us to carve out moments of clarity, inspiration, and divine connection for God.

This book isn't just about pretty pictures; it's a sacred space where our dreams and God's promises intersect. Each image has been carefully curated to reflect the richness of our spiritual journey, the depth of our Christian faith, and the beauty of our collective journey.

Imagine flipping through the pages of Vision Board Clip Art Book for Black Christian Family and seeing images that speaks deeply with your soul – images of strength, prayers, and unwavering faith. These are more than just illustrations; they're visual prayers, unending reminders of God's love, grace, and favor upon our life and family.

Vision Board Clip Art Book for Black Christian Family isn't just about looking; it's about seeing ourselves through God's eyes – as beloved children and apple of his eye, destined for greatness, and empowered to make differences in the world. It's about seeing our prayer lives take shape, our prayers answered, and our lives transformed by the power of faith.

So, beloved Christian family, as you journey through these pages, let your hearts be open, your spirits be lifted, and your dreams take flight. Let the images within this book be your companion on your spiritual journey, your confidants, and your road map for growth.

With joyful hearts, let's embrace the vision God has placed in our hands, for in him, all things are made possible and we can do all things through him that strengths us.

With love, hope, and blessings.

Acknowledgment

We extend our heartfelt gratitude to every beautiful black Christian family who has joined in this sacred journey of faith and vision. Your presence and participation have infused our Vision Board Clip Art Book for Black Christian Family with an abundance of hope, inspiration, and divine purpose. Each page holds God's guidance, encouraging you beyond your wildest thoughts into His overflowing blessings. May every clip art serve as a testament to your divine purpose

Together, we celebrate the power of faith and the beauty of God's promises manifested through each curated clip art and heartfelt prayer. Your support, thought, reviews and feedback means the world to us, and your unwavering faith have truly made this endeavor a blessing beyond measure.

With love and appreciation,

Steps on How to Create a Vision Board

Step 1: Gather Your Materials:

"Vision Board Clip Art Book for Black Christian Family", poster board, corkboard, or canvas, scissors, glue or tape, markers or pens

Step 2: Find a quiet and peaceful environment where you can focus.

Play some soft worship music or inspirational hymns to set the atmosphere.

Step 3: Take your time to flip through the clip art images in the book.

Pay attention to the clip art images that resonate with you spiritually and emotionally.

Step 4: Select clip art images from the book that align with your chosen theme.

Step 5: Carefully cut out the selected clip art images from the book.

Arrange the images on your poster board or canvas in a way that feels visually appealing and meaningful to you.

Don't forget to leave some space for affirmations, manifestation or Bible verses.

Step 6: Use markers or pens to write down affirmations, prayers, or Bible verses that complement the images on your vision board.

Step 7: Once you're happy with the arrangement, glue or tape the clip art images and words onto the board securely.

Step 8: Take a moment to sit back and reflect on your vision board.

Offer a prayer of gratitude to God for His guidance and provision in your life and family.

Ask for His continued blessings and guidance as you and your family pursue your individual dreams.

Step 9: Find a prominent place in your home where you can display your vision board.

Make sure it's somewhere you all can see it every day to keep you focused and motivated.

Step 10: Take time regularly to review your vision board and reflect on your progress.

Update it as needed with new goals, aspirations, or insights that arise along your journey.

Remember, your vision board is a powerful tool for manifesting your dreams and aligning with God's purpose for your life. Stay faithful, stay focused, and watch as He works wonders in your life.

Faimly

Psalm 133:1):
Lord, help us to live together in unity as a family, for it is good and pleasant in Your sight.

Psalm 91:10):
Lord, we pray for your protection over our family. Guard us from all evil and keep us safe under the shadow of your wings.

A family that prays together stays together.

Ash Wednesday
Season of Renewal

Turn to God
Repent, Fast and Pray

ISAIAH 58:6
AS WE FAST AND PRAY, WE ARE EMPOWERED TO FIGHT AGAINST INJUSTICE AND STAND FOR FREEDOM AND EQUITY.

SPIRIT LEAD ME

Alsmgiving
Fasting
Praying

Consider how you want to live this Lent.
Present yourself to God in prayer

PSALM 51:17
IN OUR VULNERABILITY AND REPENTANCE, WE FIND GOD'S UNFAILING LOVE AND MERCY.

THE EMPTY TOMB PROCLAIMS GOD'S POWER TO TURN OUR DARKEST MOMENTS INTO STORIES OF TRIUMPH, REVEALING HIS UNWAVERING LOVE FOR US.

ON THIS GOOD FRIDAY, WE EMBRACE THE DEPTH OF GOD'S LOVE POURED OUT ON THE CROSS FOR US.

ON THIS BLESSED DAY, WE LIFT UP PRAYERS OF THANKSGIVING FOR ALL THE BLESSINGS YOU HAVE BESTOWED UPON US, DEAR GOD.

F orgiveness

A cceptance

S elf-control

T ruth

I ntegrity

N ourishment

G race

Trust in **HIS** Timing
RELY ON HIS PROMISES
Wait for **HIS** Answers
Believe in **HIS** Miracles
Rejoice in **HIS** Goodness
Relax in **HIS** Presence

AS A FAMILY, WE CELEBRATE THE VICTORY OF LIGHT OVER DARKNESS, OF HOPE OVER DESPAIR.

I WILL Praise **HIM**
I WILL Ask **HIM**
I WILL Thank **HIM**

HE DIED FOR ME

I LIVE FOR HIM

NEXT TIME YOU WANT TO QUIT.

REMEMBER: HE WAS
BETRAYED, BROKEN, TORTURED, THIRSTY, TIRED,
BLEEDING AND ABOVE ALL NAILED TO THE CROSS
FOR OUR SAKE.

ONLY ONE GOD
ONLY ONE WAY
ONLY ONE SAVIOR

JESUS
CHRIST

MY FAMILY AND I ARE REDEEMED BY THE BLOOD OF JESUS CHRIST.

A GREE WITH GOD

M OVE WITH GOD

E END WITH GOD

N EVER DOUBT GOD

CONNECT TO GOD

THE PASSWORD IS:

PRAYER

PALM SUNDAY

PALM SUNDAY

Celebrate The King

Matthew 21:9
WE RAISE OUR VOICES IN PRAISE AND THANKSGIVING, ACKNOWLEDGING THAT WE ARE BLESSED AND HIGHLY FAVORED, FOR WE ARE PART OF A GLORIOUS KINGDOM HERITAGE.

John 12:13
WITH OPEN ARMS AND JOYFUL HEARTS, WE CELEBRATE THE KING OF KINGS, TRUSTING IN HIS DIVINE GUIDANCE AND PROTECTION.

Psalm 118:26
OUR FAMILY STANDS BLESSED AND UNITED, ALWAYS MOVING FORWARD IN THE LIGHT AND LOVE OF THE LORD.

FAITH
F orwading
A ll
I ssues
T O
H eaven

GROW
G O to church
R ead your Bible
O bey what you read
W itness

JESUS CHRIST IS THE **ANSWER** TO EVERY PROBLEM IN MY LIFE

STUDY YOUR BIBLE BECAUSE SATAN STUDIES YOU

IF GOD BRINGS YOU TO IT: HE WILL BRING YOU THROUGH IT

PREPARE YOUR HEART FOR JESUS

OUR HOME IS A SANCTUARY OF WARMTH, LAUGHTER, AND SPIRITUAL GROWTH, BLESSED BY GOD'S PRESENCE.

WE NURTURE OUR CHILDREN IN THE WAY OF THE LORD, PLANTING SEEDS OF FAITH THAT WILL GROW FOR A LIFETIME. (INSPIRED BY PROVERBS 22:6)

UNITY AND LOVE ARE THE CORNERSTONES OF OUR FAMILY, GUIDING US IN ALL OUR RELATIONSHIPS. (INSPIRED BY PSALM 133:1)

GOD'S PROMISES ARE OUR FAMILY'S INHERITANCE, GUIDING US THROUGH EVERY SEASON.

WE ARE A FAMILY ROOTED IN FAITH, RISING ABOVE ADVERSITY THROUGH GOD'S GRACE.

AS A FAMILY, WE EMBRACE GOD'S CALL TO JUSTICE, PEACE, AND LOVE IN OUR COMMUNITY AND BEYOND. (INSPIRED BY MICAH 6:8)

WE ARE A FAMILY ROOTED IN FAITH, RISING ABOVE ADVERSITY THROUGH GOD'S GRACE.

JOSHUA 24:15: BUT AS FOR ME AND MY HOUSEHOLD, WE WILL SERVE THE LORD.

PRAY

PRAY.
MANIFEST.
HUSTLE.
THANK GOD.
REPEAT.

MY GOD
IS ABLE.

PRAY.
BELIEVE.
RECEIVE.
MATTHEW 21:22

MY FAMILY AND
I ARE
GRATEFUL
LORD

IN MY FAMILY,
GOD GETS THE
GLORY

JUST A SMALL FAMILY WITH A BIG GOD

BIBLE STUDY

FAMILY DEVOTION

WORSHIP GOD

PRAISE HIM

REJOICE IN THE LORD

AFFIRMATIONS

Our home is filled with love, peace, and God's presence

We walk by faith, not by sight

We are blessed and highly favored by the Lord.

Our family is a testament to God's love and grace

We are the head and not the tail, above and not beneath

God's plans for us are to prosper and not to harm

We stand united in faith and love.

The joy of the Lord is our strength

Every day is a gift from God, and we cherish it together.

We are warriors of light, spreading love and peace

Our bonds are strengthened by God's unending love.

In all things, we give thanks to the Lord.

Our legacy is built on faith, hope, and love

We overcome obstacles through faith & perseverance.

THERE IS POWER IN THE NAME OF JESUS

HOLY SPIRIT

RAIN ON MY FAMILY

AND GOD DID IT!

I CHOOSE G.O.D
Greatest Over Darkness

THE GRACE OF GOD IS NOT A LICENSE TO SIN.

MY FAMILY ARE CARRIERS OF GOD'S GLORY

THE STRUGGLE IS REAL, BUT SO IS GOD

LIFE WITH JESUS ONLY GETS BETTER.

MY FAMILY DID NOT GET LUCKY, WE PRAYED A LOT.

LORD REMOVE ANY SEED OF BITTERNESS IN MY FAMILY.

IN EVERY SITUATION, PRAY!

NOT TODAY SATAN

A FOOL FOR JESUS

THE FATHER THE SON & THE HOLY SPIRIT

CHRIST DIED FOR OUR SIN

REVELATION 5:5 THE LION OF THE TRIBE OF JUDAH HAS PREVAILED

JOHN 10:9 I AM THE DOOR. IF ANYONE ENTERS BY ME, HE WILL BE SAVED AND WILL GO IN AND OUT AND FIND PASTURE.

LION OF THE TRIBE OF JUDAH

THE LION OF JUDAH ROARS WITHIN MY FAMILY, GIVING US COURAGE & STRENGTH TO FACE WHATEVER LIES BEYOND EACH OPEN DOOR.

OPEN UP, ANCIENT DOORS, AND LET THE KING OF GLORY ENTER. PSALM 24:9

ISAIAH 22:22

ELOHIM

HOLY ONE

YAHWEH

KING OF KINGS

ALMIGHTY

GODFIDENCE

EL OLAM

EL ROI

EL SHADDAI

TIME to STUDY

Faith

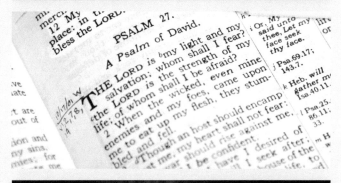

BIBLE STUDY

♥ PRAY & WORSHIP ♥

Holy Bible

FAMILY FUN ACTIVITIES
FAMILY GATHERING

FAMILY TRAVEL

Bible Verses When You Feel:

Grief/Sorrow
2 Samuel 1:1-12
Nehemiah 1:1-11

Afraid
John 14:27
Psalm 23
Psalm 27:1
2 Chronicles 20:15

Depressed
Psalm 130
Isaiah 61:3
1 Kings 19:1:9
Psalm 42:5-11

Disappointed
Proverbs 23:18
Romans 5:4-5
1 Peter 2:6

Needs Forgiveness
Acts 3:19
Isaiah 1:18
Daniel 9:9
1 John 1:19
Matthew 6:14-15

Needs Encouragement
Matthew 6:14-15
Proverbs 3:5-6
Isaiah 41:10
John 14:27

ATTRIBUTES

1. https://www.freepik.com/free-photo/christ-crucified-cross_879734.htm#page=2&query=jesus%20risen&position=45&from_view=keyword&track=ais&uuid=fa591b6f-ae5d-42e6-9995-a36311005989

2. https://www.freepik.com/free-photo/still-life-crown-thorns_25212112.htm#fromView=search&page=1&position=41&uuid=6ad360b6-18ef-4258-8ea8-b0ba0405f6d3

3. https://www.freepik.com/free-photo/cross-christianity-collage_94959024.htm#query=jesus%20tomb&position=10&from_view=keyword&track=ais&uuid=3fb5cbc9-ba84-453c-b4bf-10a49b1c0b5b

4. https://www.freepik.com/free-photo/view-christian-cross-with-water-background_66464936.htm#page=2&query=jesus%20tomb&position=6&from_view=keyword&track=ais&uuid=6e1c046b-1ef0-4f43-9c1f-8f423835130c

5. https://www.freepik.com/free-vector/ash-wednesday-event-with-leaves_7041796.htm#fromView=image_search_similar&page=1&position=0&uuid=e6a7773b-4229-4b03-8ad5-b5a2b5ab0634

6. https://www.freepik.com/free-vector/easter-illustration-with-heavenly-light-cloud-background-he-is-risen-christian-religious-design_24711325.htm#query=jesus%20background&position=2&from_view=keyword&track=ais&uuid=9f521b3c-c069-4f98-9347-eccdf0700b42

7. https://www.freepik.com/free-vector/watercolor-background-religious-ash-wednesday-celebration_133479280.htm#query=easter%20cross&position=16&from_view=keyword&track=ais&uuid=82c781f7-96e2-4d48-99ba-f88ee406434b

8. https://www.freepik.com/free-photo/view-christian-cross-with-water-background_66464962.htm#page=4&query=jesus%20tomb&position=0&from_view=keyword&track=ais&uuid=e9e248e8-b61d-43b0-b592-059f73b32ebd

9. https://www.freepik.com/free-photo/god-christian-faith-collage_94958937.htm#from_view=detail_serie

10. https://www.freepik.com/free-photo/god-christian-faith-collage_94958942.htm#fromView=search&page=1&position=28&uuid=e4b93ee9-e5fd-4f6a-bb18-4c52587b2ae7

11. https://www.freepik.com/free-vector/realistic-background-palm-sunday_138557874.htm#fromView=search&page=1&position=3&uuid=d1002832-38a3-4d3e-ae06-701d225ef79f

12. https://www.freepik.com/free-vector/christian-cross-congratulations-palm-sunday-easter-resurrection-christ-vector-illustration-eps10_12590619.htm#query=easter%20cross&position=0&from_view=keyword&track=ais&uuid=179be936-e672-4293-b353-94432ffbcba9

13. https://www.freepik.com/free-vector/flat-he-is-risen-easter-sunday-lettering_23873046.htm#fromView=search&page=1&position=4&uuid=77c55c2e-e635-4b28-85cf-0eb2ce98f1a9

14. https://www.frccpik.com/free-vector/lettering-god-stickers-collection_30555368.htm#fromView=search&page=2&position=9&uuid=0f8fd360-05bd-42fd-b877-e4da13ec72d5

15. https://www.freepik.com/free-vector/traditional-good-friday-holy-week-poster-design_25453662.htm#fromView=search&page=1&position=45&uuid=cc53444b-3867-4460-99c0-49eff5ac9b1a

16. https://www.freepik.com/free-photo/holy-communion-concept-with-bible_24236990.htm#fromView=search&page=2&position=26&uuid=068b42d0-3fac-4f6e-a600-4d4fcacf9398

17. https://www.freepik.com/free-photo/cross-christianity-collage_94959023.htm#fromView=search&page=1&position=30&uuid=2fb0c896-2dd3-4637-a8b2-338dca500750

18. https://www.freepik.com/free-photo/christian-cross-nature_49656226.htm#fromView=search&page=1&position=0&uuid=3a19bdfd-5348-45f1-b23f-09262c6603e6

19. https://www.freepik.com/free-vector/faith-religion-stickers-lettering-template_35585815.htm#fromView=search&page=4&position=3&uuid=0f8fd360-05bd-42fd-b877-e4da13ec72d5

20. https://www.freepik.com/free-vector/monochrome-easter-lettering-stickers-collection_37447025.htm#fromView=search&page=1&position=19&uuid=f917a986-df01-4e28-87c4-259f790c019d

21. https://www.freepik.com/free-photo/close-up-women-holding-hands_13948914.htm#fromView=search&page=1&position=13&uuid=c0fe3dc4-ec41-414f-b96b-33f6c753e88b

22. https://www.freepik.com/free-photo/happy-family-silhouette-sunset_8380524.htm#query=family%20together&position=14&from_view=keyword&track=ais&uuid=05535b7c-6e42-43ef-9950-094bf65cc881

23. https://www.freepik.com/free-photo/embraced-african-american-family-talking-kitchen_29453526.htm#page=3&query=family%20together&position=14&from_view=keyword&track=ais&uuid=5f2ee587-a9ef-44a5-992c-8c9cb6b7c798

24. https://www.freepik.com/free-vector/christian-cross-congratulations-palm-sunday-easter-resurrection-christ-vector-illustration-eps10_12590623.htm#fromView=search&page=1&position=0&uuid=2fb0c896-2dd3-4637-a8b2-338dca500750

25. https://www.freepik.com/free-photo/holy-bible-with-rays-light-coming-out-ai-generative_41369556.htm#fromView=search&page=2&position=30&uuid=daa5ffdd-9db7-4477-af11-de88f406fc10

26. https://www.freepik.com/free-ai-image/view-3d-lion-with-nature-background_67214555.htm#page=3&query=lion%20king&position=26&from_view=keyword&track=ais&uuid=b38313bd-5f13-4642-a60d-a9e09435115e

27. https://www.freepik.com/free-photo/portrait-lion-ai-generated_47072733.htm#fromView=search&page=1&position=0&uuid=de2a583a-cc87-47f9-9962-a92b4fc645a3

ATTRIBUTES

28. https://www.freepik.com/free-photo/front-view-modern-family-retro-style_49656712.htm#query=family%20table&position=24&from_view=keyword&track=ais&uuid=a5ac6f9d-5810-4004-94f9-1a3b217c3023

29. https://www.freepik.com/free-ai-image/free-photo-good-friday-background-with-jesus-christ-cross_40380793.htm#from_view=detail_alsolike

30. https://www.freepik.com/free-ai-image/3d-rendering-jesus-neon-cross_68013473.htm#query=redemption&position=11&from_view=keyword&track=sph&uuid=062c0e94-2733-42f2-a958-c1d82f1ca9f8

31. <a href="https://www.freepik.com/free-photo/holy-bible-with-rays-light-coming-out-ai-generative_41369556.htm">Image by chandlervid85</a> on Freepik

Made in the USA
Columbia, SC
12 September 2024

42230415R00027